BATS!

MYSTERIOUS AND MISUNDERSTOOD MAMMALS

by Lydia Lukidis

CAPSTONE PRESS
a capstone imprint

Published by Capstone Press, an imprint of Capstone
1710 Roe Crest Drive, North Mankato, Minnesota 56003
capstonepub.com

Copyright © 2026 by Capstone. All rights reserved. No part of this publication may be reproduced in whole or in part, or stored in a retrieval system, or transmitted in any form or by any means, electronic, mechanical, photocopying, recording, or otherwise, without written permission of the publisher.

Library of Congress Cataloging-in-Publication Data is available
on the Library of Congress website.
ISBN: 9798875216817 (hardcover)
ISBN: 9798875216824 (paperback)
ISBN: 9798875216831 (ebook PDF)

Summary: Some people are scared of bats. But these fascinating nighttime fliers are one of the world's most misunderstood animals. Young readers will learn about the features and behaviors of bats and why it's so important to protect these marvelous mammals.

Editorial Credits
Editor: Carrie Sheely; Designer: Heidi Thompson; Media Researcher: Jo Miller; Production Specialist: Tori Abraham

Image Credits
Alamy: Avalon.red, 15; Getty Images: ©Juan Carlos Vindas, 23, istock/Buzun Maksimilian, 12, iStock/Chelsea Sampson, 28, istock/CraigRJD, back cover (top right), 18, McDonald Wildlife Photography Inc., 13 (little brown bat), Nicolas Reusens, 13 (vampire bat); Science Source: James H. Robinson, 17, MerlinTuttle.org, 8, 11, 22, USFWS, 26; Shutterstock: Andrey Prokopenko, 1, 6, (bats), Anton Starikov, 16, Beth Ruggiero-York, 29 (bottom), crystaldream, 29 (top), Deliciosa, 29 (middle), Eric Isselee, 24, grayjay, 14, Gulf MG, 7, Henner Damke, 21, Jeff Reeves, 19, Jishith Jayaram, 27, MisterStock, 6 (speech bubble), Photoongraphy, 4-5, PITOON KITRATANASAK, 13 (painted bat), Roberto Dani, 13 (ghost bat), Rosa Jay, 31, Rudmer Zwerver, back cover (top left, bottom left), 3, Sapodorado26, 13 (Honduran white bat), Worraket, front cover; Superstock: Christian Ziegler/Minden Pictures, 10, Ingo Arndt/Minden Pictures, 13 (epauletted fruit bat), Jared Hobbs/All Canada Photos, 25, Michael Durham/Minden Pictures, 20, 31

Design Elements
Shutterstock: incrediblephoto, Max_Lockwood

Any additional websites and resources referenced in this book are not maintained, authorized, or sponsored by Capstone. All product and company names are trademarks™ or registered® trademarks of their respective holders.

TABLE OF CONTENTS

BUSTING BAT MYTHS.............. 4
BATS AROUND THE WORLD 10
BAT BEHAVIOR 14
SMALL ANIMALS WITH BIG ROLES ... 22
BAT CONSERVATION............... 26
GLOSSARY 30
READ MORE 31
INTERNET SITES............. 31
INDEX 32
ABOUT THE AUTHOR........... 32

CHAPTER 1
BUSTING BAT MYTHS

The hike is taking longer than you thought. You quicken your pace. The sun has set and it's getting dark. Shadows of tall trees line your path. Suddenly, you hear a strange sound.

WHOOSH!

Where is it coming from? You look around. An endless stream of bats flies out of a cave. You watch as hundreds of them flap their wings furiously. You duck and cover your head.

IT'S NOT WHAT YOU MIGHT THINK!

Many people see bats as bloodthirsty creatures. They might think bats are gross. They may get scared if bats fly too close to them. Others worry bats may bite them. They think bats might give them a disease called rabies.

But bats don't deserve the bad reputation they get. They are not usually dangerous and rarely bite humans. Plus, they are helpful to us. They eat millions of insects that can be pests. Bats help the environment too. Let's learn more about these amazing creatures!

BAT TRIVIA

Check out these trivia questions and brush up on your bat facts.

1. Do most bats suck blood?
No! There are more than 1,300 species of bats. But only three species drink the blood of animals. They are all types of vampire bats.

2. Are bats blind?
No! This is a common misconception. Their eyes are small, but they can see.

3. Do all bats sleep upside down?
No! Most bats sleep upside down. But a few bat species sleep inside the leaves of trees.

4. Do bats carry rabies?
Yes, they can. But less than 1 percent of bats carry the disease.

5. Bats are rats with wings.
No way! It's true that bats are small and furry. But they're not related to rats or mice. Bats are not even rodents.

AWESOME WINGS

We know bats fly. Does this mean they are birds? Nope. Bats are mammals. They're the only mammal in the world that can fly.

Bats belong to the mammal group Chiroptera, which means "hand wing." Bat wings are like hands. Each wing has a thumb and four fingers, just like people's hands do. Sometimes bats scoop up food with their wings. Their wings are not made out of feathers. They are folds of skin.

FACT
Every bat has a furry coat, right? Wrong! There are a few hairless species.

A CLOSER LOOK AT BATS

Bats have some things in common, such as sharp teeth and wings. But they also have many differences depending on their species. For example, bats are different sizes. The flying fox is the biggest bat in the world. Its body is about 16 inches (41 centimeters) long. The Kitti's hog-nosed bat is the smallest bat in the world. Its body is about 1 inch (2.5 cm) long.

Bats' coat colors have variety. Bats often have shades of brown, gray, or black on top. They may have lighter shades underneath. Some bats have stripes. In South Sudan, there's a rare striped bat. It has bold black and white stripes.

The size of bats' ears varies too. Spotted bats have gigantic ears. Their ears can be up to 1.6 inches (4 cm) long. This is about one-third of the bat's body length. The bat rolls its ears around its head when resting.

Spotted bat

BATS VS. OTHER MAMMALS

Bat
- **Diet**: is a carnivore that eats only meat or an herbivore that eats only plants, depending on the species
- **Life span**: 10–30 years
- **Reproduction**: gives birth to live pups, one to four at a time
- **Most active**: at night

Giraffe
- **Diet**: herbivore
- **Life span**: 15–25 years
- **Reproduction**: gives birth to a live calf, usually one at a time but twins are possible
- **Most active**: during the day

Red Fox
- **Diet**: is an omnivore that eats both meat and plants
- **Life span**: 2–6 years
- **Reproduction**: gives birth to live pups, four to six at a time
- **Most active**: at night

Lion
- **Diet**: carnivore
- **Life span**: 10–14 years
- **Reproduction**: gives birth to live cubs, one to six at a time
- **Most active**: at night

Platypus
- **Diet**: carnivore
- **Life span**: 12–20 years
- **Reproduction**: lays eggs, one to three at a time
- **Most active**: at night

Human
- **Diet**: omnivore
- **Life span**: 70–75 years
- **Reproduction**: gives birth to live babies, usually one at a time, but multiple babies are possible
- **Most active**: during the day

CHAPTER 2
BATS AROUND THE WORLD

In Mexico, a bulldog bat soars through the air. It scans the sea for prey. Aha! It spots a juicy fish.

The bat swoops down. It drags its large, hooked claws into the water and grabs the fish. It gathers the fish into its wings. Chomp! It bites into its prey, devouring it within seconds.

A bulldog bat swallows a fish in Panama.

Nearby, a vampire bat flies out of a cave at night. It approaches a farm and spots a chicken. The bat lands near a sleeping chicken and slowly inches toward it. The bat bites down with its razor-sharp teeth on the chicken's leg. Blood oozes out. The bat licks the blood with its long tongue. The chicken doesn't even wake up.

The three species of vampire bats are the common vampire bat, the hairy-legged vampire bat, and the white-winged vampire bat. These bats feed on the blood of animals such as cows, horses, or birds. They need half an ounce of blood each night. But they rarely bite humans.

What do other types of bats eat? Most bats are insectivores. They feast on insects. Some bats eat small animals such as birds, frogs, and lizards. Others eat plant parts such as fruits, leaves, flowers, and seeds. Some eat nectar and pollen from plants.

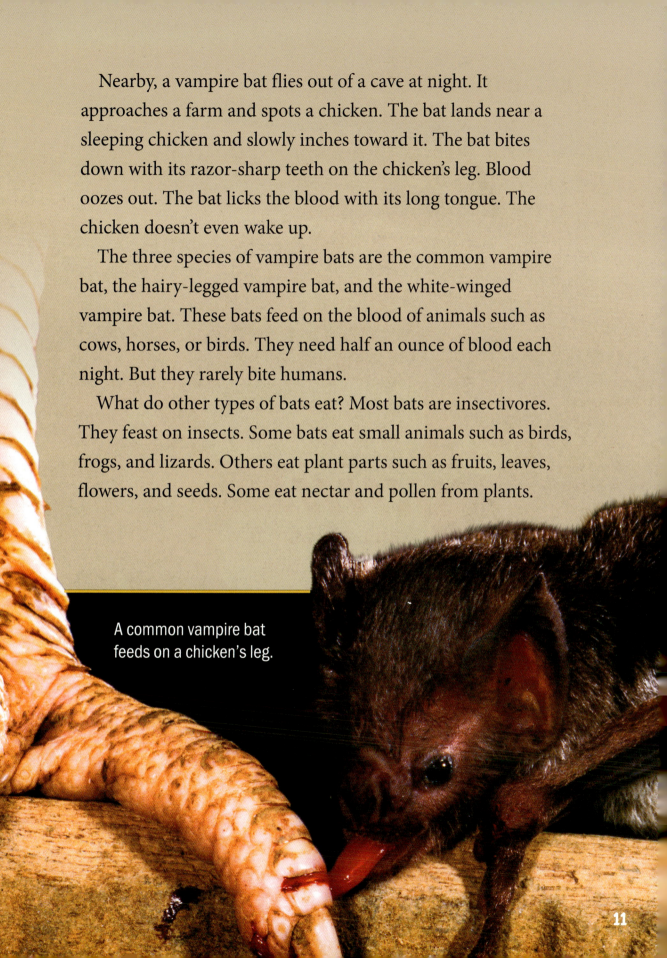

A common vampire bat feeds on a chicken's leg.

BAT, BATS, EVERYWHERE!

Bats are almost everywhere around the world. But they can't survive in extreme cold. They don't live in the Arctic or Antarctica.

Bats live in different habitats. You can find them in rain forests. Others live in deserts or near oceans.

Bats live in homes called roosts. They spend the day in roosts and sleep there. Female bats also give birth there.

Bats might make their homes in barns, attics, or caves. Bats may also choose to live in hollow trees or buildings. These shelters keep them safe from predators. They also protect the bats from bad weather.

Pond bats roost in a cave.

MEET SOME BAT SPECIES!

Name of bat: Honduran white bat
Where it lives: South America
What it eats: fruits and vegetables
Fun fact: It lives in the leaves of trees.

Name of bat: painted bat
Where it lives: Asia
What it eats: insects
Fun fact: It is orange with black on its wings. Some people say it looks like a butterfly.

Name of bat: Buettikofer's epauletted fruit bat
Where it lives: Africa
What it eats: fruits
Fun fact: The adult male has a big snout with large lips.

Name of bat: little brown bat
Where it lives: North America
What it eats: insects
Fun fact: It can eat half of its body weight in insects every night.

Name of bat: common vampire bat
Where it lives: Central and South America
What it eats: the blood of mammals and birds
Fun fact: It can walk, run, and jump.

Name of bat: ghost bat
Where it lives: Australia
What it eats: large insects, frogs, birds, lizards, and small mammals
Fun fact: It has super hearing. It can hear insects and animals moving on the ground up to 65 feet (20 meters) away.

CHAPTER 3
BAT BEHAVIOR

The moon shines in the night sky. A bat flies through the air. The bat starts following a moth. It spreads its wings around the insect. There's no escape now! The bat gulps down its prey.

How do bats see at night when it's dark? Bats find their prey using echolocation. They make high-pitched sound waves. These sound waves bounce off objects around the bats. Then the sounds return to the bats' ears. The bats recognize their own calls. The echo helps them figure out the size and shape of objects near them.

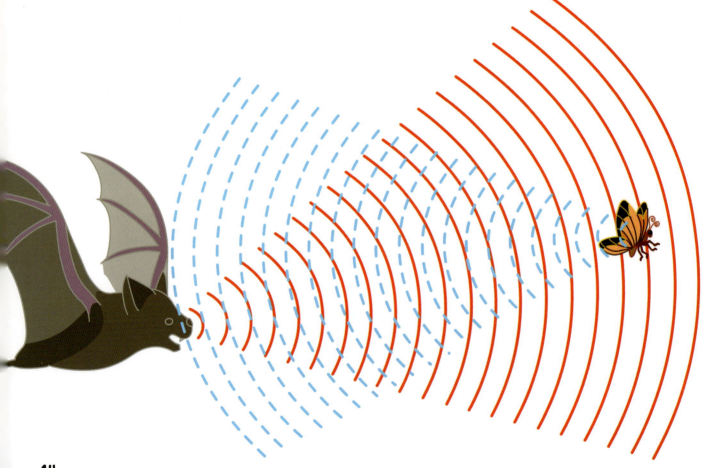

Echolocation is not just for hunting. It helps bats find their way around and avoid obstacles.

Bats make other sounds to communicate. They chirp, screech, and purr. They may use these sounds to look for a mate. The sounds can even show emotion. Some scientists think bats might use echolocation as a form of communication too. Many of these sounds are ultrasonic. They are so high-pitched humans can't hear them.

FACT
Bats aren't the only animals that use echolocation. Whales, dolphins, a few birds, and some shrews also use echolocation.

EXPLORE ECHOLOCATION

This activity will help show you how echolocation works. You need only a few supplies. Let's get started!

What You Need:

- two people
- baking sheet or pan
- 2 long cardboard tubes (from paper towels or wrapping paper)
- blindfold, such as a dinner napkin or a bandana

What You Do:

1. Each person will use a cardboard tube.
2. Place a metal baking sheet against a wall.
3. One person talks or whispers through their paper tube, directing their voice at the baking sheet.
4. The other person is blindfolded and holds their tube to their ear, also pointing it at the baking sheet.
5. Now remove the sheet and try to communicate. What do you notice?

How Did It Work?

The person's voice was louder when the baking sheet was there. That's because the sound waves bounced off the sheet and returned as an echo. When there was no baking sheet, the sound waves didn't return. It was harder to hear the other person talking.

Hairy-legged vampire bats

Bats are nocturnal. They hunt at night and rest during the day. When you go to bed, they might be just leaving their roosts.

We don't usually see bats during the day. There are more dangers for bats. It's easier for predators to find and eat them.

Bat Myths and Folktales

There are many myths and folktales about bats. Most don't paint bats in a positive light. Bats' unique features and their nocturnal behavior might have given them a mysterious reputation. This could have led to their inclusion in stories.

One folktale comes from India. It's about some unhappy birds that prayed to become human. But their dream didn't fully come true. They were given ugly half-human faces. They were also given hair and teeth. But they kept their wings. They were no longer birds, but they weren't human either. This made them ashamed. They hid during the day and only came out at night.

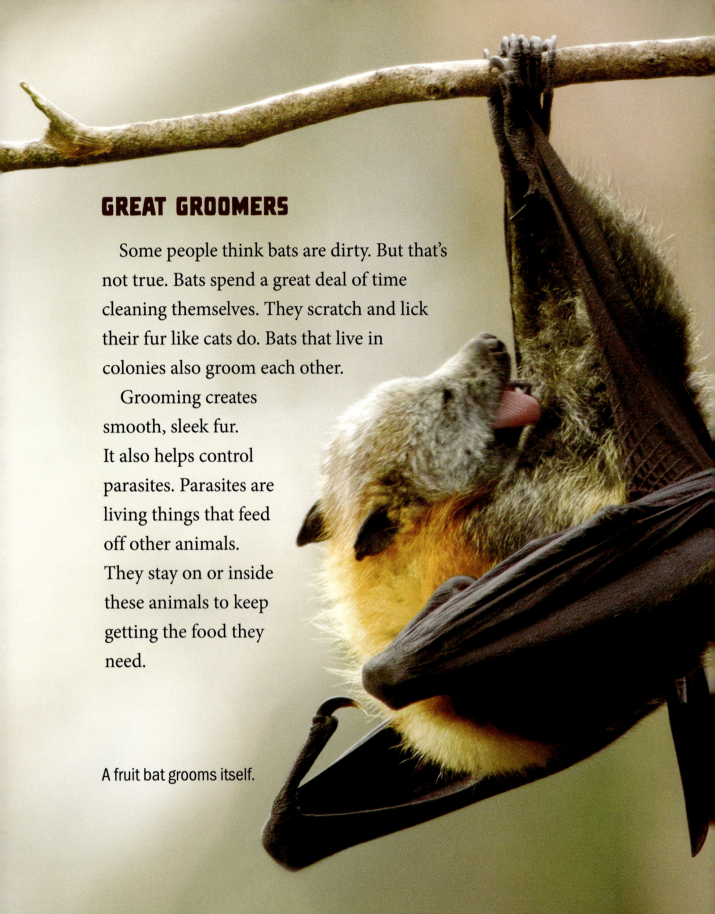

GREAT GROOMERS

Some people think bats are dirty. But that's not true. Bats spend a great deal of time cleaning themselves. They scratch and lick their fur like cats do. Bats that live in colonies also groom each other.

Grooming creates smooth, sleek fur. It also helps control parasites. Parasites are living things that feed off other animals. They stay on or inside these animals to keep getting the food they need.

A fruit bat grooms itself.

FLEXIBLE AND FAST

Some bats live alone, but most live in colonies. If you spot one, you can usually expect to see more nearby. Some colonies are small. Others can have millions of bats. The world's largest colony is in Bracken Cave in Texas. More than 15 million Mexican free-tailed bats live there.

Bats are most active in the spring and summer. Some species hibernate in winter. They rest to save energy as they hibernate. Others migrate in winter. These bats fly to another area that is warmer and has more food.

Do bats fly fast? They sure do! But they don't fly the same way birds do. Birds have rigid wings that move only in a few directions. Bat wings have more than 24 joints. For this reason, bats have more agility and control as they fly.

FACT
Cheetahs are the fastest animals on land. They can reach speeds of 75 miles (121 kilometers) per hour. But bats are the fastest mammals! The Mexican free-tailed bat can fly up to 100 miles (161 km) per hour.

Mexican free-tailed bats leave Bracken Cave in Texas.

BAT SUPERPOWERS

Did you ever hear the expression "blind as a bat"? It's not true, because bats can see well. Bats have the same senses as humans. They can see, hear, feel, smell, and taste.

Some of their senses are better than ours. The leaf-nosed bat has amazing night vision. It's almost as good as a person's while wearing night-vision goggles.

Bats can detect and respond to the motion of air over their wings. This sense helps them fly with precision. They have touch sensors on their wings. These are called Merkel cells. Scientists discovered that the sensors help the bats feel and respond to slight changes in airflow. The sensors connect to the brain of the bat, which controls its movement.

PRECIOUS PUPS

Baby bats are called pups. They weigh about one-third their mother's weight. Bats give birth between May and July. Most species give birth to one pup. Sometimes more than one pup is born.

Pups drink milk from their mother for a few months. By three weeks old, they learn how to fly. They then can hunt for food.

Bats usually live 10 to 30 years. One Brandt's bat in Siberia lived until at least age 41 in the wild!

A flying fox bat with its pup

CHAPTER 4
SMALL ANIMALS WITH BIG ROLES

Bats help us by eating loads of bugs. Many insects destroy plants and crops. Bats act as a natural pest control for them. This means farmers don't have to use as many pesticides. Bats save farmers more than $3.7 billion per year.

All of those bugs need to move through a bat's digestive system. That means a lot of poop! The poop is called bat guano. You would probably want to stay away from it. But some people collect it! They place a plastic sheet on the ground at the entrance of a roost. Bats often poop as they enter their roost. The guano is collected and packaged. Farmers put some in the soil. It's a great fertilizer. It gives the soil vitamins and helps plants grow.

In Cambodia, farmers collect guano under artificial roosts and sell it as fertilizer.

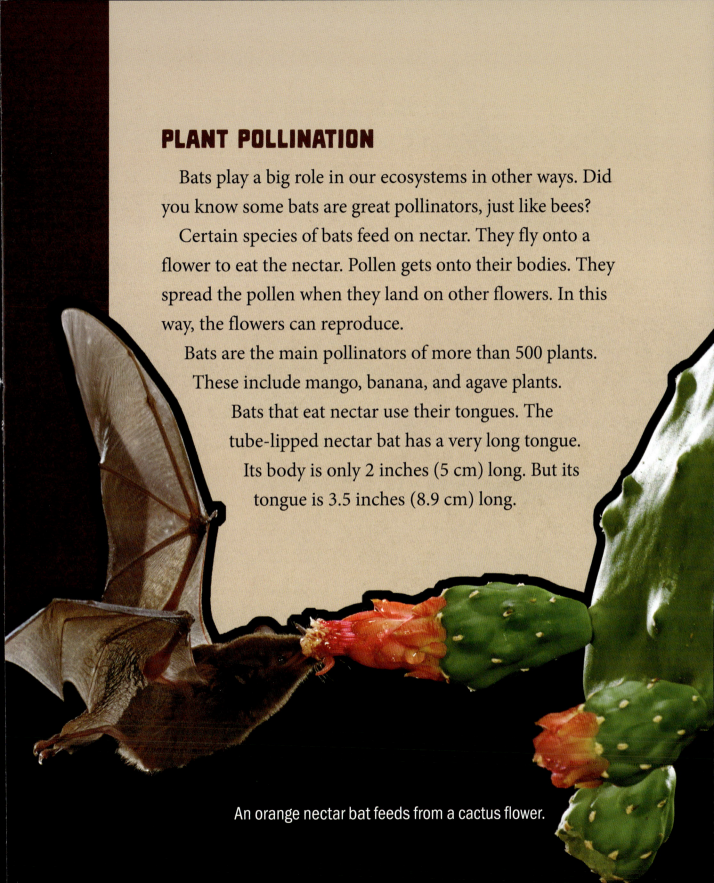

PLANT POLLINATION

Bats play a big role in our ecosystems in other ways. Did you know some bats are great pollinators, just like bees?

Certain species of bats feed on nectar. They fly onto a flower to eat the nectar. Pollen gets onto their bodies. They spread the pollen when they land on other flowers. In this way, the flowers can reproduce.

Bats are the main pollinators of more than 500 plants. These include mango, banana, and agave plants.

Bats that eat nectar use their tongues. The tube-lipped nectar bat has a very long tongue. Its body is only 2 inches (5 cm) long. But its tongue is 3.5 inches (8.9 cm) long.

An orange nectar bat feeds from a cactus flower.

SCATTERING SEEDS

Wildfires, floods, and plant diseases destroy many forested areas each year. In some places, bats can help reforest these areas.

Fruit-eating bats scatter the seeds of plants. They eat fruit and swallow the seeds. The seeds go into their poop. Then when they poop in another area, the seeds get into the soil. More trees and other plants grow from the seeds.

CLUES FROM BATS

Scientists often monitor bats. Why? Bats are indicator species. That means they can tell us if something has changed or is going to change in their habitat. Scientists look for clues to see how pollution, climate change, and other factors affect the bats.

Bats are very sensitive to changes in their habitat quality. Their presence normally shows that an ecosystem is healthy. But if their population decreases or they change their habits, it warns scientists that something is wrong. For example, observing bats can warn us when a disease starts spreading. Scientists can then take action. They can prevent a disease outbreak. Whatever affects bats might also affect other animals.

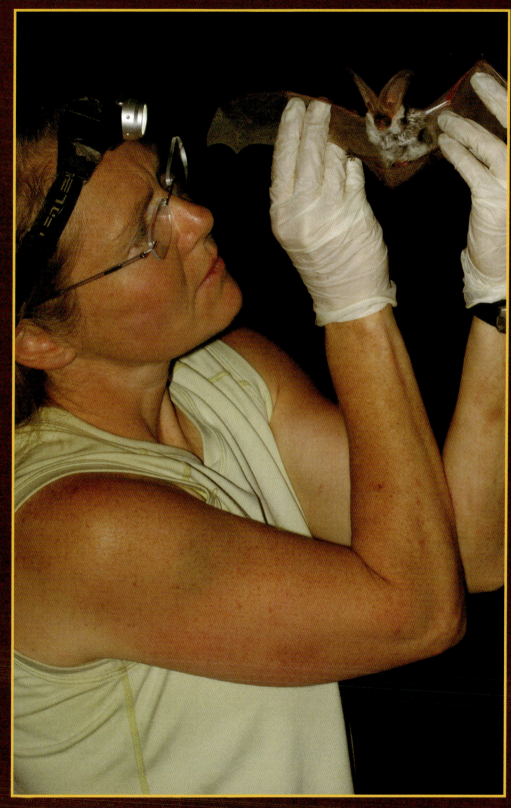

A scientist studies a spotted bat in Canada.

CHAPTER 5
BAT CONSERVATION

In 2006, scientists observed bats in a New York cave. They found white splotches on many bats. The bats were sick. What was happening? The scientists did tests. That's how they discovered white-nose syndrome.

White-nose syndrome is caused by a fungus. It looks like white fuzz. It's mostly found on the nose and other hairless parts of bats, such as the wings. The disease spreads in cold, damp places where bats hibernate.

The infected bats wake up often because the fungus hurts their skin. That makes them use their fat reserves. As a result, many bats starve before spring comes.

The disease spreads fast. Since 2006, 6.7 million bats in the United States and Canada have died because of it. Scientists are trying to find cures and treatments.

What can we do to help? If you ever visit a cave, it's best to clean your shoes and gear before and after entering the cave. If you ever see a bat in the wild, leave it alone. Don't touch it.

A bat with white-nose syndrome

Deforestation has occurred in India, which has destroyed animal habitats.

HOW HUMANS AFFECT BATS

What other threats do bats face? Their biggest threat is us.

Humans cause habitat destruction. We cut down forests to build homes and roads. We build malls and other buildings. We cut down forests to plant and grow crops. When we do this, bats and other animals lose their homes.

We also make climate change worse through pollution. For example, our homes and cars use a lot of power. Burning fuel in gasoline-powered cars and heating our houses releases a greenhouse gas called carbon dioxide. Greenhouse gases trap heat in our atmosphere, causing climate change. Even what we eat and how much we throw away adds to greenhouse gas emissions. This affects all animals, including bats. Rising temperatures change migration and hibernation patterns of animals. Studies show how some bat species move around in relation to the weather.

FACT
Sometimes bats are hunted by humans and eaten. People in Africa and Asia eat bat soups and other dishes with bat meat.

BE KIND TO BATS

There are many other threats to bats, such as wind turbines. These turbines turn the power of wind into electricity. But they have massive blades. Each year, about 1 million bats crash into the turbines and die. Researchers are trying to find safer ways to place and use turbines.

Cats are a threat too. Many bats are killed by cats each year.

Bats sometimes roost in people's houses or on their property. Some people kill these bats. In many places, killing bats is illegal.

It's important that we conserve as many bats as possible. Female bats usually raise only one pup per year. It's hard for them to grow their population when so many are killed.

YOU CAN HELP!

There are many organizations around the world that help with bat conservation. They work with governments to create better laws to protect bats. These laws can control deforestation and restore habitats. Sadly, many countries don't protect bats enough.

There are ways you can help too. Understanding these amazing animals is the first step. Do more research and then spread awareness in your community. You can share what you learn with family and friends. Or you can choose bats as a topic for school projects. You can also celebrate Bat Week.

So next time you're on a hike at dusk and see a bat swoosh by, don't be afraid. Remember, bats help us in many ways!

MAKE A BAT-FRIENDLY BACKYARD OR GARDEN

You can help bats by attracting them to your backyard. To build a bat-friendly backyard or garden, remember the three basic needs of a bat.

yucca

Food

First, make sure the bats have food. If the bats in your area eat insects, it's easy. Don't use pesticides in your garden. Don't mow the lawn too much in an area. Leave dead and decaying leaves on the ground. You can also create a pollinator garden with flowers for bats that drink nectar. Add plants that bloom at night, such as agave, evening primrose, or yucca.

bat box

Shelter

You can build or buy a bat box. The bats can roost in it. Instructions for building a bat box can be found online or in books. You will need an adult to help you.

Water

You can supply bats with water. Since bats drink by swooping down as they fly, they need at least 7 to 10 feet (2.1 to 3 m) in length of water. Be sure to replace the water regularly.

GLOSSARY

colony (KAH-luh-nee)—a large group of animals that live together

echolocation (eh-koh-loh-KAY-shuhn)—the process of using sounds and echoes to locate objects

ecosystem (EE-koh-sis-tuhm)—a system of living and nonliving things in an environment

environment (in-VY-ruhn-muhnt)—the natural world of the land, water, and air

fungus (FUHN-guhs)—a single-celled organism that lives by breaking down and absorbing the natural material it lives in

hibernate (HYE-bur-nate)—to spend winter in a deep sleep; animals hibernate to survive low temperatures and lack of food

mammal (MAM-uhl)—a warm-blooded animal that breathes air; mammals have hair or fur; female mammals feed milk to their young

migrate (MYE-grate)—to travel from one area to another on a regular basis

precision (pri-SI-zhuhn)—being exact or refined

predator (PRED-uh-tur)—an animal that hunts other animals for food

prey (PRAY)—an animal hunted by another animal for food

rain forest (RAYN FOR-ist)—a thick forest or jungle where at least 100 inches (254 cm) of rain falls every year

species (SPEE-sheez)—a group of plants or animals that share common characteristics

READ MORE

Drimmer, Stephanie Warren. *Ultimate Mammalpedia.* Washington, D.C.: National Geographic Kids, 2023.

Murray, Laura K. *Why Do We Need Bats?* North Mankato, MN: Capstone, 2024.

Riskin, Dan. *Fiona the Fruit Bat.* Vancouver, British Columbia, Canada: Greystone Kids, 2022.

INTERNET SITES

National Geographic Kids: 10 Brilliant Bat Facts!
natgeokids.com/uk/discover/animals/general-animals/bat-facts

National Geographic Kids: Vampire Bat
kids.nationalgeographic.com/animals/mammals/facts/vampire-bat

The Nature Conservancy: Amazing Facts About Bats
nature.org/en-us/about-us/where-we-work/united-states/arizona/stories-in-arizona/top-10-bat-facts

INDEX

climate change, 24, 27
coat colors, 8
colonies, 18, 19
conservation, 28

diets (of bats), 11
diseases, 24, 26
   rabies, 5, 6
drinking blood, 6, 11, 13

echolocation, 14, 15, 16
environment, 5

guano, 22, 24

habitats, 12, 24, 27, 28
hibernation, 19, 27

Merkel cells, 20
migration, 19, 27
myths, 6, 17

pesticides, 22
pollination, 23
pollution, 24, 27
predators, 12, 17
pups, 9, 21, 28

rabies, 5, 6
roosts, 12, 17, 22, 28, 29

seeds, 11, 24
species, 6, 7, 8, 9, 11, 13, 19, 21, 23, 24, 27

vision, 6, 20

wind turbines, 28
wings, 4, 6, 7, 8, 10, 13, 14, 17, 19, 20, 26

ABOUT THE AUTHOR

Lydia Lukidis is an award-winning author of more than 50 children's books. At the tender age of 6, she began reading and writing. She loves all animals, including bats, and her eternal curiosity led her to study science. Today, she incorporates her studies in science into her work and loves writing about STEM topics. Her book *Deep, Deep, Down: The Secret Underwater Poetry of the Mariana Trench* (Capstone, 2023) is a Crystal Kite winner, Forest of Reading Silver Birch Express Honor, and Cybils Award nominee. Lydia lives in Montreal, Canada, with her daughter, who also loves science. For more information, visit her website at www.lydialukidis.com.